W9-BJT-713

FROM SINNER TO SAINT

ERIC D. COONEY

BALSAM BOOKS

For further information, please contact:
www.balsambooks.com

Book designed by:
Arbor Books
19 Spear Road, Suite 301
Ramsey, NJ 07446
www.arborbooks.com

Printed in the United States of America

From Sinner to Saint
Eric D. Cooney
Memoir

1. Title 2. Author 3. Memoir

Library of Congress Control Number: 2007902861

ISBN-10: 0-9675854-2-2
ISBN-13: 978-0-9675854-2-0

*I want to thank my mother, Peggy, without whose love
and support this book would not exist.*

*This book is dedicated in loving memory to my father,
David O. Cooney*

FOREWORD

In August of 1991, my junior year of college, I traveled to Spain for a 'semester at sea'—actually, two semesters. I had recently declared English as my major, and it was my aim, first, to enhance my overall language skills by mastering a second language, and second, and perhaps even more importantly, *to broaden my horizons; to SEE THE WORLD.*

Things were going just fine; then, after approximately three and a half months in Granada, it hit me: the scenery was different, my classmates were of different nationalities, everyone was speaking Spanish, or, in some of our cases, at least attempting to, yet...*GOING TO SCHOOL IN SPAIN WAS JUST LIKE GOING TO SCHOOL IN AMERICA!*

That was when my disillusionment began.

One night in mid-October, sitting in the tiny bedroom at my host family's apartment and lamenting, "Even my friends here in Spain are just like my friends in America!," I carved into my notebook: "Heaven help me!"

Little did I know...

BOOK I
THE GRANADA GROUP

CHAPTER 1

"C'mon. He's interesting," she said in that irrestistible little girl's voice of hers.

Jane led me to *The Pilar del Toro*, a luxurious open-air restaurant tucked behind Plaza Nueva.

When we got there, the eccentric-looking man I'd met casually at *The Castanneda*, a cozy bar down the street, was propped against the far wall with an intense but welcoming expression on an otherwise poker-player's face.

Before we even had a chance to sit down, the man, David, was telling us about how he'd received three 'signs,' something about three different-colored flowers at the next table. The signs, he said, had to do with us joining his 'school.'

David had mentioned his school when we'd met at *The Castanneda*, and though I'd found the idea of it somewhat intriguing then, I was still only half-ready to sign up.

David must have sensed my hesitation. Nevertheless, he said, "Think about it. It could be what you're looking for and then some."

I looked at Jane, who was unusually silent.

As if reading our minds, David said, "C'mon, aren't you guys looking for *something else*?

Jane and I nodded simultaneously.

"Well then…" David stopped talking and concentrated on his cafe con leche.

He must have seen the two of us thinking over our lives. How could he have known that, just days before, Jane and I had been sitting in Plaza Triunfo after class discussing this very thing: *how empty we felt,* how we longed for *something more?*

David told us that in his school, people learned a technique, a type of meditation that, if done properly, could *stop time.*

Although my interest in the technique was moderate at best, it spoke to my search for a way to fill up the emptiness, or depression as I called it, inside of me.

"C'mon, try something new," David was saying. "It's seven mil (pesetas) a week. You can continue for as long as you want. A month…a year…"

Jane and I looked at one another. We hadn't known that what David was proposing would cost money. Not that it didn't seem reasonable, but perhaps because we felt, or had been *conditioned to believe* that "spiruality should be free."

As David smoked a Ducado, his favorite brand of Spanish cigarette, he gave us a mini lecture on *"Why."*

Basically, he was poor. But that wasn't the only reason.

David had a more important kind of wealth: *spiritual weath;* a *SOUL.*

He also had something called will-power, he said.

"When you guys get done with your fate," he said, "you'll have will-power. In the meantime though, the seven mil a week is for *loaning* you mine."

"For now, he concluded, "it's a partnership: You have spiritual needs; I have physical needs. Pretty simple, right?"

"Right," Jane and I agreed.

Our lives were about to change, David said. "You guys found me, all by yourselves."

I didn't know precisely what he meant by that, but I was sure it was not just "a line."

David walked with us halfway across Plaza Nueva and we said goodnight.

As we departed for our respective dwellings, David gave us one final nugget of encouragement: "You're officially off the *law of accident* and under the *law of fate,*" he said.

CHAPTER 2

David and his girl, Deliana, were living on the floor of an antique shop run by a local millionaire, Fernando Something-or-other. This is where Jane and I first came for our daily lessons.

In our first session, David spoke about, and later demonstrated, his technique "for conscious rebirth."

He asked us if we'd ever read the books of Carlos Castaneda.

"Kind of," we said (Jane had a copy of C.C.'s first book, *The Teachings of Don Juan*).

"Well," David said, looking at each of us straight in the eye, "have you ever heard stories of near-death experiences?"

"Sure," we concurred.

David continued, "At the moment of death, according to Don Juan, our awareness is *consumed*; it's *taken* from us.

David paused and took a long drag of his Ducado.

"The intention of the technique I'm going to show you is to avoid death," he went on, "to *keep* your awareness."

"If you complete your recapitulation…" he began, "I promise you you'll be at least ten years younger than your physical age, and maybe, maybe—get this, you won't have to die at all!"

"Sounds pretty groovy right?"

We smiled.

Before demonstrating "Recapitulation," David gave us these instructions: "You can tell people *Why* and *What*, but not *How*."

The technique turned out to be surprisingly simple, at least in theory. It was basically a breathing and visualizing exercise, the purpose of which was SEEING THE TRUTH.

I felt I was part of a private club now. I even saw visions of myself 'recaptulating'—that's how David said it—back in America; changing or evolving; basically impressing the world.

CHAPTER 3

David liked to talk. In fact, he talked almost constantly. I couldn't get a word in edge-wise and pretty soon, I stopped trying altogether.

He was wise. He had a glow about him.

He also smoked a lot; he said that tobacco was *mental energy*.

"You'll have to recaptulate cigarettes," he said, "everything you 'know' about smoking: your aunt that died of cancer; all of that. Unless…no, you *have* smoking imprints."

"What's an imprint?" I asked.

We were sitting on an old oriental rug, on the floor of his room in the back of the shop. The walls were chipping and the rug was torn in places. David warmed his hands on the iron heater, the cheap kind all the electricians' shops sold.

"What's an imprint?" he began. "Basically, an event happens. Your mother tells you, "Take a bath"; you see your parents having sex; some kid steals your favorite baseball mit, whatever. You have a physical experience—okay, it could be a mental one I suppose—and an emotional reaction to it."

That's just basic psychology, I thought.

David went on to say though, "Sounds simple, right? Hey, these imprints can be real buggers. Anyway," he explained, "that's what recaptulation's for—to recapture these moments in your life."

David's eyes lit up then. "It's not exactly the experience you're trying to recapture, although, yeah, maybe at first; it's the unconscious or subconscious *meaning* of the experience."

As a final note, he added, "That's why you sometimes have to go over the same imprints until you get your energy back."

I liked to hear David talk, the way he touched on all subjects as we sat around the shop or at the neighborhood bar adjacent to it.

I liked the way David smoked unabashedly.

I also really liked—and I never entirely figured out the reason for this—the way David *walked*. As he strode, or glided, down *Calle Real*, the main artery connecting *The Realejo* with Plaza Nueva, his long hair streaming behind him, his head and chest high, the *Granadinos* milling along the narrow avenue—mostly teenagers and old ladies doing their daily grocery shopping—didn't so much seem to acknowledge him, but rather, to *feel* him.

CHAPTER 4

"Where are you from?" Jane asked David one day at the shop.

"Springfield, New Jersey," David said.

I almost doubled over laughing at the ridiculousness of this. I realized that he was serious, but it sounded too unreal. *Springfield, New Jersey?*

I was surprised, too, that David had given us a straight answer this time, because that first day at *The Pilar*, when Jane had asked him, "How long have you been in Spain?" David had responded, "Six years."

We later found out…get this…it was actually TEN!

All of this intrigued me for the following reason: I'd been reading the chapter in Castaneda's third book, *Journey to Ixtlan*, about "making oneself inaccessible." In the chapter, Don Juan tells Carlos, "Personal power is a commodity." He goes on to say that giving away too much information, or the wrong kind of information, can drain one's personal power.

Did David care about 'Personal power'? I knew he believed in a lot of the same things as Don Juan, and I was sure that he at least understood a fair amount about *control,* for one thing.

Not until years later, though, would I realize that David's awareness went much deeper. David, at that time, was probably already enlightened! As an adept, David had, much like Don Juan, perhaps to an even greater extent than D.J., a healthy dose of the Saint in him.

But even today—because although he said then that he'd read all thirteen books of Castaneda's, he never, to my recollection, mentioned "Personal power"—I still wondered, *Did David somehow miss that chapter?*

CHAPTER 5

One of the first things David did after we joined his school was to send me and Jane to the beach. David didn't tell us which beach to go to. Our only assignment was: "Sit down with a glass of wine at some point and, in an hour, tell each other your life's stories."

The trip to the beach—we chose Almunnecar—was magical. As we sat in the sand (it was a little cold for swimming), it occurred to me that the beach had a similar effect on me as that of LSD. I told Jane, who had never taken the drug, "This is what it's like." It was a lot like being a kid, I realized, something about that state of innocence.

We told our life stories over a glass of wine, as David had recommended, and in the morning, I 'made my move.' Jane reciprocated, and the long-awaited romantic component of our relationship was born!

When we returned from the beach, it must have been obvious that we'd connected. David made a comment to this effect and though we would tell him we hadn't 'gone all the way,' he said, "Yeah, yeah, you made love."

CHAPTER 6

David had referred several times to Deliana's psychic abilities. He was psychic too, he told us. But he talked now about how the two of them communicated with higher beings *together*.

He said it was necessary for a female psychic to "have a man around."

"Some of them get really messed up," he explained.

"Why do they have to have a man?" Jane asked.

"Why do they have to have a man?" David said, smiling at Deliana. "Well, when I first met this little elf, she was open to everything. But a higher mental center," he continued, "is necessary to make knowledge practical. Deliana can talk to God on her own now, but she still likes to have me around, to formulate questions. Isn't that true Elf?"

Deliana half-smiled.

"A man needs a woman too," David went on. "I'm not crazy about being mediumistic, even if I *could* do what Deliana does. I'd rather be a higher mental genius," he said.

"What's a higher mental genius?" I asked.

"A higher mental genius sees patterns," he explained. "Basically, it's the seventh chakra, if that means anything to you?"

I tried to assimilate everything David said. His words made sense, but I was still a little lost.

It seemed David was done talking for the moment; he and Deliana were having some sort of silent communication (they were raising their eyebrows at one another and moving their lips in a playful sort of way. Flirting, I guessed).

Finally, I piped up, saying, "How do you ask a question?"

I felt this was a "flimsy" thing to say, but, without missing a beat, David said, "Hey kiddo, wanna call up Dad for a minute?"

David turned to me, said, "Normally, I wouldn't do this; it's not for show, but fine…just this once."

Deliana, who was wearing pink bunny slippers and had long braids in her hair, sat down on the tattered rug, closed her eyes gently, and crossed her legs.

"Ready?" asked David, who was crouching nearby her now.

"Um-hmm," she hummed.

"Okay," David said, turning to me. What do you want to know?"

I thought for a minute, then somewhat shyly, said, "Why am I here?"

"Here in this shop?" David chuckled, "or here on Earth?"

"Earth," I said.

David scratched his chin. "Well, if you really want to know…"

He thought a moment longer, then looked over at Deliana.

"C'mon," he finally said, "Isn't there something more practical on your mind?"

I thought again, long and hard this time, while the others all waited patiently.

"Well," I said, "it's sort of like…What should I do?"

"Okay," David smiled, "Good, I hear you."

Settling back on the rug and warming his hands on the iron heater, he related, "Well, last night Deliana and I were working on you guys, and the Higher Beings said you had some talent for painting.'"

David paused for half a minute or so and let the 'news' sink in; then he asked me, "So, what do you think?"

"It sounds great," I said.

"Sounds fantastic is more like it, right?"

CHAPTER 7

Eventually, Jane and I got an apartment with David and Deliana. It was small and unfurnished, but once we found furniture—"They don't have flea markets here, so people just throw stuff away, perfectly good stuff," David said—and fixed it up, the apartment became more than livable.

"This is a far cry from the floor of the shop," David said.

I was happy for him, but also mildly—secretly—disappointed. *A true Guru should live in squalor*, I thought to myself.

I painted every day; it was my thing now. I usually divided my time between outdoors and the shop. I often spent a couple hours sketching 'in the field,' then returned to *The Realejo* to paint.

One day, Deliana came over to my desk to look at my painting of the 'Neptune Fountain.'

"Wow, that's great!" she said.

"It's okay," I replied.

She started to walk away.

"What did I say?"

"You should learn how to take a compliment," was the response.

I realized instantly she was right and I went back to my canvas.

That night, while David and Deliana were at The *Ocanna* having coffee and Jane and I were alone in the shop, I asked her to pose for me briefly.

She said okay, and I got out my drawing pad. Jane was slimming down from dancing. I fumbled for my charcoal and began making preliminary lines, light lines at first, then, once I had the contour down, heavier, bolder strokes. Then I began working the shadows inside the lines, putting down scratches and smearing them until they were the right value. I put shadows under the breasts and armpits, the chin and the inside of the abdomen, trying to make the marks neither too hard nor too soft. I finished off with the soft shadows, those on the face and arms. I didn't draw much of the legs. The highlights came last and were done with an eraser.

As always, I wasn't satisfied with what I had done, but I was learning and having fun.

CHAPTER 8

It wasn't always easy being around David and Deliana. Besides being much better artists than Jane and me, they were spiritual people. They told the truth, and the truth sometimes hurt. I was continually aware of my, what David called 'receptivity,' and Jane cried whenever she became honest. David had been up front with us, saying, "It's not easy to evolve; that's why it's good to have a guide."

Still, we felt ashamed in front of our now 'old friends' from school, and didn't know what to tell them about what we were doing. They seemed to think it was some sort of cult; "The School of David," one girl called it half-sarcastically. There was a rift between us now. We lived in two different realms.

I sometimes pitied myself for being so young. I was in a difficult situation. I felt I was abandoning something – school, a straight path, the socially accepted path – in favor of something glamorous, mystical, and above all, unpredictable. When it came right down to it, I was surprised at how easily I had chosen that more unknown way. David's charm certainly had a lot to do with it, but it was more than that.

CHAPTER 9

The four of us were like a happy family, grooving along.

David and I would usually go to the shop together in the 'morning' (3:00 or 4:00 in the afternoon actually, with our 'energy schedule').

One day, David asked me how my painting was coming. I said I was still having trouble finishing the fountain picture.

"Yeah, Virgos," he said with an understanding gleam in his eye. "C'mon, I'll give you some help. Tonight, after I practice, we'll hunt down that varmint."

My previous painting, "The Golden Gate Bridge," David said, was "related to 'transmission'." I was sure he would find similar meaning in the much more elaborate fountain. *But would I see it?* I wondered.

At eight o'clock, true to his word, David led the way to Plaza Bibrambla, where we walked in a wide circle around the fountain, checking it out from every angle. David took a long look at it, then said that the lower level, with its gargoyles and fishes – "Those guys are weird!" he said – was the unconscious; the middle represented earth; and the uppermost, the planets, was heaven.

I was impressed by his certainty and by the observations he made. He'd commended by choice of subject several weeks ago, and now said I was at 'Point 8,' *Before Completion* (See the *I Ching* for further explanation).

I fed off David's enthusiasm for the project, and the next day I was finished.

"It deserves a place in Fernando's *taller*," David said.

I was proud. My first *real* painting.

CHAPTER 10

It was Spring and lent was approaching. In Spring, David explained, "People's buffers come off. Everybody gets a little boost."

"You've been running," he said to me. "You look good. Jane looks good too. Maybe we'll even go vegetarian for spring-cleaning."

After a short discussion about purification; about what foods we could eat ("What about Tuna?" I asked hopefully), we listened to David explain what he called 'Eagle's Command.'

He said that everyone felt it (Eagle's Command) and that they (people) instinctively knew "what they should do." It almost sounded like he was saying God spoke to us, but that wasn't quite it.

"It's really *your* command," David said. "Don Juan didn't even believe in God. No one's going to tell you exactly what to do. It's a *chance* basically.

David's explanation seemed clear to me, and at the same, confusing. At the end of our little talk though, I found myself inspired, grateful to be there. The little uncertainty I felt was balanced out by my faith in him and Deliana, and by having Jane with me.

CHAPTER 11

Ever since we'd known him, David had been making references to Romeo and Lisbeth, or Liza, the couple now in Germany who had 'stolen his car.'

He had painted a rather dark picture of his 'runaway' students; he called Romeo "a murderer" and said that he "did it for the girl."

Romeo and Liza were larger than life to me and Jane, like a couple mysterious characters from a romance—or horror—novel.

David had once said, "For every student we have, we get ten 'potential students.' Since we had known D & D, there had been a few of these potentials, but so far our immediate school consisted of just the four of us. David's remarks about Romeo and Liza had instilled a morbid fascination in us. The prospect of meeting these renegade students who had come before us was almost too much excitement for me and Jane to handle.

Just when I thought it was all a hoax David had made up for some 'educational' reason, I found myself at the door of the shop one bright April morning, face to face with the the long-lost Europeans. His arm wound tightly around the blonde-haired Swiss, who was every bit as pretty as David had said, Romeo, a cool, dark figure with long, almost jet-black hair, asked me with a piercing look, "Is David here?"

I thought about saying, "Wait here," and going to get David myself, but instead, I found myself leading the couple through *The Realejo* and into our neighborhood.

Just as we rounded the corner by the *Placeta del Toro* fruit stand near our house, David appeared.

He came down the street, casual as can be, stopped abruptly, and said to Romeo and Liza, "What's up?"

Romeo and Liza followed David down the street. Instead of coming along, I ran up to our house, burst through the door, and, seeing Deliana, who was busy chopping vegetables, blurted out, "Romeo and Liza are here! Romeo and Liza are here!"

CHAPTER 12

We didn't see much of Liza and Romeo at first. They were working out their karma on daily walks. David had already decided how they would repay him for stealing the car. In addition to returning the car, they had agreed to pay 'damages.' They were also confessing everything sinful they'd done *since* stealing the car.

Liza, who was close in age to Deliana, a couple of years younger, seemed, from what I could gather, to be having trouble with the teacher/student dynamic (Deliana was facilitating Liza's confession and David, Romeo's), and giving Deliana a hard time, i.e. whining a lot.

I was already aware that Deliana wasn't crazy about the teacher role. She had complained to David on a few occasions regarding Jane. David gave her pep-talks, talking about it (teaching) being part of her fate. He had even mentioned the Higher Being they called "Mom," saying, "Don't you think she had to teach some?"

David and Deliana didn't try to hide information about Romeo and Liza's confessions from Jane and me. There was an underlying feeling that the work they did with Romeo and Liza was exactly that: work. Besides projecting the feeling that there was nothing to hide, I felt that they, especially David, wanted me and Jane to witness how they worked. He had talked early on about how it was our fate to become like him and Deliana one day.

They alternated between discussing what had gone on in Liza'a and Romeo's confessions, and asking questions, as they came up, to "Mom and Dad." David's questions were always very well formulated. He usually seemed to have an idea of the answer already; Deliana's 'asking' seemed more like a way of *checking* whatever hypothesis he had.

It was clear to me that David really had Romeo and Liza's best interests in mind. It's wasn't punishment to confess; it was for purity. I felt this so clearly that I began to become jealous of the attention Romeo and Liza got.

My emotions didn't slip by David. "Hey Eric," he called to me from the kitchen where he and Deliana were working one night, "Are you jealous of Romeo and Liza?"

I didn't know what to say. I couldn't deny it, but I was too ashamed to admit it."Well, I can't protect you if you're jealous," he said. "They're not clean yet. Don't you get it—they envy *you guys*. There's nothing to be jealous of, understand?"

"Yeah," I croaked.

Deliana and David went back to their work. I sat at my desk looking at the Edvard Munch book I'd brought back with me from Oslo, where Jane and I had been in December during our month-long European 'tour.' *It's all too much, this evolution,* I thought. *Painting will keep me grounded I hope.*

CHAPTER 13

It was Thursday night. Jane and I returned late from the shop. Deliana had a picnic basket ready and David said we were going to the Hot Springs. It was the first time he'd driven his car since getting it back. Deliana 'talked to it' to make sure it was alright. We drove along the highway, then down a long country road that wound through several tiny towns. I hadn't been into the Spanish countryside much. The rolling hills and rows of olive trees alternated between pitch dark and the bright light of the moon. *What a perfect night for an adventure,* I thought.

We finally came to the stone entrance of the *Alhama Baths.* The road was bordered by cliffs. At the end was a small parking area. It was dark as the cliffs blocked the moon.

David wasted no time and made straight for the baths, trusting that we would follow him. The baths were very hot but we soon got used to them. I looked at Jane. She was beaming and looked elfin. D& D were acting like two children, splashing and frolicking and sliding between the two pools, laughing all the while.

After a nice soak, we ate the picnic dinner Deliana had packed: hard-boiled eggs, bread, jam, pickles, avocados, and, to top it off, chirimoyas, a Spanish fruit that tastes a lot like…vanilla ice cream.

"Deliana talked to a chirimoya one time," David said. "What was it kiddo? Joy?"

Deliana nodded her head.

No one talked much on the way home. We were all pleasantly relaxed. I felt like putting my arm around Jane, but I still felt a bit awkward doing that—cuddling—in David and Deliana's presence.

We got back to the house around 2:30 in the morning. Jane and I made love and stayed up until around 4:00.

Sometime early in the morning, perhaps 5:00, Jane and I were simultaneously awakened by something. Or rather, we were both still asleep, in some kind of a nightmare, experiencing the exact same fear.

Something was after us. Jane was running for the door, trying to escape. I yelled to her, but my voice had no sound. She heard me somehow anyway, and came back to the bed. Then we just clung to one another for about half an hour.

"What was that?" Jane finally said.

"I don't know," I gasped, "but I felt like it wanted my soul."

This is more or less what I told David two days later. The first thing he said was, "Why didn't you guys tell me about this sooner?"

I just shrugged.

"Do you feel like it got you?" he asked.

I almost said yes, but instead I said, "I don't know."

Finally, Jane burst out, "What was it? Do you know?"

David hesitated for a second, then said, "Well, my guess would be Romeo."

"Romeo? really?" Jane choked.

"Yeah, or his demons."

"Why?" she said.

"He envies you guys. You're young, you're new. Now you'll have to really be careful."

"How come?" I asked.

David started to say something, then stopped. He seemed uncertain about what to tell us. I thought I had some idea of what he was about to say, but I was wrong.

"Just act as normal as possible for awhile," David said.

CHAPTER 14

I couldn't tell how serious David had taken what we'd told him. At one point, he had seemed poised to tell us more. Perhaps he would eventually. For the time being, though, I just had to trust him.

David stopped giving us direct advice. He hinted that we should use Jane's tree, the one Deliana had helped her select as a medium for receiving answers to questions it was my job to supply. We tried and tried, but the answers we received were not very clear. We were operating under fear and guilt. I already knew that these 'lower emotions,' as David called them, made it difficult to receive objective results.

It was very frustrating. At one point, Jane admitted to me she'd been thinking a lot about leaving. It was our first really big test; we were failing miserably it seemed. The day we had told David of our encounter, our nightmare, he had said, as if to himself, "You're so young."

I thought I had overheard him say to Deliana later that evening, "If life says they're ready, they're ready." But I didn't know just what this meant. Mostly I just felt rather low on energy, apathetic.

We spent most of the week alternating being feeling pity for ourselves and making feeble attempts at communicating through the tree. Finally, on Thursday night, we went to the teashop. We sat down at a booth near the back of the shop and ordered tea. One thing about the teashop: we at least felt at home there. Maybe something would happen.

As we were thinking this, David and Deliana came in. They didn't acknowledge us at first; they sat down in the alcove, or nook, in the middle of the long entryway.

We felt their presence and wondered what they were discussing. We'd been struggling all week, and David, although he hadn't been unkind in any way, had avoided us for the most part. I imagined that he had forgotten us by now. I didn't flatter myself that he was thinking about us, but the possibility gave me hope nevertheless. All of a sudden, he appeared at our table.

"Still pretty down huh?"
"Yeah," I said.
"Well, do you have any hope?"
I didn't say anything, just shrugged my shoulders.
"What about the tree? Any luck?" he asked.
"Some," Jane said.
"Well?"
"I think it told me to leave."
"That's just your fear and your blame," David guffawed. "Isn't there something better you can think of? I thought you wanted to be a dancer. I *know* Eric wants to be a painter."

David thought for a minute, then said, "Romeo, I mean Kindler—that's what I'm calling him now, Kindler—has a strong force. I was hoping you could use what Deliana and I have given you: art, mediumship, higher beings, to reduce this 'mighty power' of Kindler's…it's petty jealousy. That's why I told you to 'just do your thing.'" He paused for a moment and took a long drag of his cigarette. Then, reiterating his thought, he said, "That's why I told you to just do your thing."

It all sounded so simple the way David said it. I wondered why I hadn't framed it this way. Finally, I realized that as much as I loved the *idea* of painting, higher beings, consciousness and all that, I barely had a foothold in this new world.

"Is there anybody you trust?" David was saying to us.

Jane and I both looked at him.

"Is there anybody you have faith in?"

We both sat there for a long moment. Finally I said, "You."

Suddenly, something seemed to shift. David was on our side again. He cared about us. For the last several days, I hadn't been sure.

David agreed to help us return to ourselves. He said he knew how to do it, but he would have to ask Deliana. "We have to make love and become like our parents," he explained. "We did it once, last August."

David went to ask Deliana, who evidently agreed. Then he told us to hang out, go to the shop, come back in a couple hours.

When we returned from the shop, David and Deliana were sitting in the kitchen in bathrobes.

"What a fuck!" said David.

Deliana shot him a sideways glare.

"Sorry kiddo," said David.

I noticed a large bump on David's left leg, a protrusion I was somehow certain had not been there before. It was none of my business though, so I didn't explore the subject.

We went into the livingroom next and David and Deliana had us stand in a peculiar posture. We extended our arms at a

45-degree angle from our shoulders and spread our feet approximately 2^1/$_2$ feet apart. I awaited more instructions, but David told us to "just hold very still." They circled us once, then simultaneously slipped something over our heads. David slapped me once hard on the back, then said, "That's it."

We all went back to the kitchen and David began explaining about the amulet.

"It's for protection," he said. "It's charged. It'll give you outward freedom: If someone blames you, it'll bounce back to them at 1.6 times the force. Right, Kiddo? Anyway, it works just as long as you don't *initiate* the blame."

Deliana started a pot of coffee while David took out a cigarette.

"Anyway, you don't have to worry about Kindler or Liza any more. But don't tell them you're wearing the charms to protect yourselves from them, okay?" he said.

Finally, David discussed the tree, saying, "We were hoping you'd get a sense for who's behind it."

It was finally clear to me then that the tree really was a medium for higher beings. It made a lot of sense. But clear, accurate communication required a lot of practice. Jane and I were just beginning. We had had to rely on David and Deliana to heal us. It had worked out fine; however, I wondered how David perceived our obvious inability to make practical much of anything we'd been taught so far.

CHAPTER 15

David talked more of the Eagle's Command. All of us, including Deliana, were working on purification. I had lots of dreams, some of which David helped me analyze. He would say things to me like, "Oh, that has to do with your painting," or, "That's something to recaptulate." He was continually making things practical, or trying to, and although I couldn't always see the connections, his enthusiasm and the way his mind worked always inspired me.

On the other hand, all the talk about Eagle's Command caused me significant anxiety. I didn't know what to expect; I was supposed to achieve some sort of 'higher level' by Easter; I still didn't know how to do that.

Jane shared my dilemma. We both felt that as artists, and even as people, we were somehow below average. The perceived privilege of having two talented teachers to depend on was the only thing that kept us believing in ourselves and in our chances of becoming *like* them.

CHAPTER 16

I no longer feared Kindler and Liza. In fact, I wanted to be around them. I had been around Jane, David, and Deliana almost exclusively for several months now and I was longing for a 'change of scenary.'

Liza showed me her paintings one day (they were phenomenal — she'd been to art school) and we talked about our favorite artists: Gauguin; Monet; Dali; D'Vinci…. Kindler played guitar for us, the Flamenco songs he had perfected…almost. The girls even got up and danced! The four of us still hadn't quite gotten to know one another, but the tension that had been so prominent at our first dinner together, when Jane and I had visited *HazaGrande* for the first time, was all but gone now. Liza was more talkative, Kindler was more relaxed, Jane wasn't as intimidated, and I was more comfortable in general.

Then, one night, a week or so later, "Eagle's Command" surfaced. Apparently, Kindler had told some people in their house about it, and it had been shrugged off as "kooky-talk." The term 'normal people' came up. Normal people…people interested in, well, 'other things.'

Although Kindler and Liza spoke fairly fluent English, they often broke off into German as the conversation evolved. This of course broke the momentum. At a certain point, I felt sure Kindler and Liza were arguing about whether Eagle's Command was 'real' or not. Liza, at least, felt threatened by it somehow. She

41

said something about it being from a *Don Juan* book. In Liza's mind, this somehow cast a shadow of doubt over David as an objective (her favorite word I later found out) source of information.

When David heard about our discussion of Eagle's Command and about Liza's skepticism, he commented, "That's just Liza. She always wants 'physical proof.' What good would it do to indulge her?"

David turned to me. "If you have faith and resist becoming negative yourself, she'd probably be forced, by some cosmic law, to do the same. If you don't keep up your faith though, she'll drag you down with her doubt."

I was sure this little speech of David's was more than just 'kooky talk.' I had felt it the other night at *HazaGrande*, the temptation David was talking about.

CHAPTER 17

It was now Eagle's Command time (it changes every year; in 1994, for instance, it was exactly one week after Easter, I remember) and one of the subjects that came up was whether or not Jane and I would stay in Granada. Originally, we had planned to stay for a year. Now July was approaching. David insinuated that our lives had changed; that normal society was now something as foreign as what he called 'David and Deliana's world.' David didn't try to convince us to stay; he did talk a lot about fate.

I wondered whether the fact that Jane and I were paying him 15,000 pesetas a week between the two of us contributed to his wanting us to stay. David wasn't a money-grubbing man, that much was clear. I didn't know exactly what he wanted from us though. It was a long time before I really *knew*.

I used my long runs in the afternoon to contemplate my situation. I had told my parents I was studying with David and Deliana, painting, doing yoga. I knew, though, that they had no real conception of my actual life. Things had become more and more difficult to explain.

I had no one to confide in, therefore, except Jane. I knew that if I thought too much about splitting, David would construe it as lack of faith. I knew I was supposed to stay, take care of Jane, evolve. It was hard, though, to accept that my life was so different nine months after coming to Spain than I'd dreamt it would be!

CHAPTER 18

Somehow it was decided, most likely by David, that Liza would go back to Switzerland. Why? David told us her twin soul was there. Liza seemingly had not argued with this 'verdict.' So it was now just me, Jane, and, of course, Kindler.

For some reason, around this time, Jane began complaining that David still owed us his and Deliana's share of the rent. At first I said, "Relax, just have faith." But she began to really obsess about the subject.

The next day, she was still talking about confronting David. This time, I didn't say anything. Part of me had begun to agree with her, but another part of me still felt it was ill-advised.

We were in our room when David returned from his morning run, and before I knew what was happening, Jane had rushed to the door, asking for money.

David flipped out, saying, "You want, you want. You little creeps are lucky to be here. You want my blood too? Fine, I'll give you your rent. Now give me the charms."

There was a struggle out in the hall.

"C'mon you little shit, give it to me," David said. "It's my power. They don't belong to you."

He came into our room and walked over to me with his hand out. I gave him the charm, reluctantly.

"Now give me the key to the shop."

I did as I was told, but felt crushed. The key to the shop had really meant something to me. It had symbolized trust and equality. It had made me feel special. I was angry at Jane for wrecking everything.

I was also surprised that David had reacted so abruptly to what was, in some way, a reasonable request. Looking back though, David had warned us about this.

"If you trust me, everything will be fine and you'll get the rent each month. I'll even pay you to go to the landlord and deliver it," he'd said.

CHAPTER 19

A few days later, David decided that Jane needed to leave. "She's suffering too much," he told Deliana.

It was decided that she would go live up at the *HazaGrande* house, where Kindler, Ralf, a new student who'd recently arrived, and five other people (students and foreigners mostly) resided. I was sad that Jane was leaving, but I felt— arrogantly perhaps— that I could manage. It was awkward though, with just David and Deliana. I didn't cook and I always felt guilty when when I sat down to a meal Deliana had prepared. I tried to paint in my room, but it wasn't like the studio at the shop; it didn't have that *D'Vinci's workshop* feel.

In the evenings, David and Deliana sat in the kitchen to work on Ralf. Ralf, with his mechanic abilities, had helped Liza and Kindler steal David's car. Since coming back to Granada and settling his debt with David, Kindler had been trying to get Ralf to do the same.

Now Ralf was here. Much of David and Deliana's initial work on him involved identifying his strengths and weaknesses. With David's higher mentality and Deliana's meditation, it seemed they were able to gather information about Ralf's past lives. My understanding was that this information shed light on Ralf's present situation.

Around the same time, I found out that Ralf himself was already seeing past lives in his recapitulation. David seemed to go out of his way to 'poke me' with this, perhaps in an attempt to awaken some spark of life in me that had been on the wane ever since Jane's 'demotion.'

I still hadn't even met Ralf. I thought I'd heard David say something about him needing to lose a few pounds, but when I ran into him along with Kindler and Jane at the waterhole one day, I noticed Ralf's body was perfect! This caused me to wonder whether I had heard David wrong, or whether his words had indeed been calculated to provoke me.

I heard some more dubious things about Ralf, but blew them off for the most part. I had talked to him and he'd seemed earnest about improving himself. He had issues, but he was incredibly likeable. What impressed me most about Ralf was his ability to 'get to the point.' He was brusque at times, oafish even, but we got along very well.

CHAPTER 20

One evening, David and Deliana sat me down in our living room and asked me, "Are you comfortable here?" It seemed like a nice way of saying, "Can you find another place to live?"

David had actually met a young Spanish couple in the teashop earlier that day and discovered they were looking for a roomate. Their apartment was just up the street. I agreed to check it out, and the following day, with a little help from David, I moved my things.

I didn't actually spend much time in my new apartment. I trekked up to *HazaGrande* most days, where Kindler and Ralf helped me set up a small painting room. Kindler also gave me guitar lessons a couple times a week.

One night, Kindler took me and Jane down to *The Avellano*, an arabic-style bar near David's shop in *The Realejo*. Kindler said he had had some dreams about the two of us, dreams which indicated we were 'stuck.' He basically suggested he could guide us a bit, pick up where David left off. This proposal didn't surprise me—I even thought I had felt it coming!

Jane, surprisingly, seemed fairly relaxed during all this. She asked Kindler, almost hopefully, "What does this mean?"

"For you," Kindler said, it means dancing. And for Eric, painting and guitar, but also…you need to recapture your *bird of freedom*."

Kindler paused as he puffed on a cigarette. "You lost that, your sense of freedom."

I told Kindler, who was feeling more and more like an older brother to me by now, that I was frightened about Eagle's Command.

Kindler took a deep breath. "This is your Eagle's Command, mein freund." Taking another puff, he said, "Don't worry so much about that. The most important thing is that you need to draw, paint...and..."

"And?" said Jane.

"Well, I wasn't going to go into it," Kindler sighed, "but you guys might need to part, at least for now."

"But we *have* been apart, Jane moaned. Becoming more confrontational now, she asked, "Is that what David said?"

"That's what *I'm* saying," Kindler retorted, perhaps a little miffed about being questioned in a way perhaps...David would not have been.

Finally, Jane addressed the question on both our minds. "David said we were twin souls."

Kindler put down his cigarette and looked straight ahead, at...some 'invisible source of all answers.' Was he pondering the question, how to answer it?

Finally, he said, "I don't know about all this 'twin soul stuff.' David and Deliana might be twin souls. I don't know."

I looked at Jane. She seemed disappointed, but strangely relieved at the same time.

CHAPTER 21

With Kindler as our teacher, we no longer recapitulated; we practiced "confession."

David had once said, "Recapitulation and confession have the same goal."

One difference, at least in terms of outward form, was that confession required someone to confess *to*.

I found it, confession, extremely uncomfortable at the outset; I had the fear, natural perhaps, that Kindler, upon hearing my confession, would use it against me somehow. David would explain to me some months later, "That (your fear) is because *you've* used this type of information in a sleazy way."

For the first few weeks, I had a difficult time talking, much less telling the truth, i.e. confessing. Finally, one day, I finally made a breakthrough. Kindler, desperate to get something real out of me, suggested: "Shake things up a little: try jogging." (Normally we would sit, or stroll). Desperate myself to get it right, I trotted for awhile. There was a wonderful path above *HazaGrande*; it wound through a forest of pine trees and up a steep hillside. Suddenly something happened. A certain sin of mine appeared and I began confessing it. From that day forward, the honest emotional state I'd stumbled upon—or attained—became my 'starting point' for confession.

I continued to see David, usually at *The Castanneda*, where he occasionally asked me how Jane was, how "running confession" was going, how the house was, things like that. That David was guiding Kindler behind the scenes should have been obvious to me, but especially during the first few weeks of Kindler's 'takeover,' I hadn't been entirely sure.

David did ask me once to tell him, honestly, "How are things working with Kindler?"

I said, "They're okay."

Looking back, I would wonder if David had been considering a return to our previous arrangement, the old teaching scenario. He must have been satisfied with my answer however, because no such return occurred, at least not then.

The four of us—Jane, Kindler, Ralf, me—now controlled the entire *HazaGrande* house. Together, Kindler and I had convinced Antonio, the landlord, to rent us the entire place for 80,000 pesetas a month.

It was great to have so much space. We converted the largest room into a dance studio/music room, and we created a tai-chi area on the lower patio. Three rooms were still empty however, and we needed rent help. To make matters even more difficult, we had decided, maybe based on an unspoken suggestion from David, not to rent the rooms to just anybody. We talked about our house becoming a school; anyone who moved in had to have at least some interest in "evolution;" e.g. art. We interviewed several people and one or two seemed like viable candidates, or, at least, 'potentials.'

Then, Kindler's grandfather died and Kindler had to go to Berlin to handle the paperwork, will, etc., and receive what turned out to be a sizeable ($300,000) inheritance.

Now, not only did Jane and I stand to lose Kindler's support as our mentor, but we, along with Ralf, were faced with the challenge of renting, by ourselves, the still-empty rooms.

CHAPTER 22

Jane, Ralf, and I, with occasional guidance from David, managed not only to keep the house running while Kindler was in Germany, but we also restored furniture, did art, and worked on several projects together, including an astrological chart, something David and Deliana had 'commissioned' Ralf to construct.

The three of us really got to know one another. Apart from the occasional tension, generated, according to David, by Kindler's absence and 'the natural disharmony of the number three,' the days we spent at *HazaGrande* and later, touring Andalucia in Ralf's BMW, I would eventually dub "The Summer of Love."

We spent the Dog Days, the last two weeks in August, at a juggling festival north of Barcelona, at the foothills of the Pyrenees, where the '92 Olympics had recently been held. Ralf had met an older man, John, in Plaza Nueva a week before. John was part of a troupe of jugglers and had turned Ralf on to the gathering. The four of us made the eleven-hour trip in Ralf's car; we arrived to find several hundred hippies camping near a lake and juggling balls, pins, firesticks, even chairs!

On the way home from the trip, I felt content. The road trip was exactly what I needed. I felt we were in harmony, even with Kindler, who had recently sold his grandfather's estate and would be returning soon.

I was excited to continue a bicycle-fixing project I had begun and through which I was learning about mechanics as well as *finishing.*

Jane started dancing again, and Ralf was refinishing—stripping and staining—a desk (another David 'commission'); he was also studying the *I Ching* and working on a version—a less intense version—of recaptulation.

Though none of us saw much of David now, we felt his presence in everything we did. He had given us this life somehow, a life of "living for oneself," a life of freedom. Perhaps we didn't think of him enough; it was one of those times, though, where everything seemed to work fine; the feeling seemed to be, *We don't need 'Big Daddy' looking over our shoulders all the time.*

CHAPTER 23

David did show up occasionally, and his presence always made us more aware of ourselves, for better or for worse. I often wondered what he and Deliana were doing now that they were, at least temporarily, out of the teaching business.

One night in late September, Ralf and I bumped into David at *The Castanneda*. He was drinking *Vino Dulce* (Sweet Wine) at the walnut bar and he told us he'd just been talking to a housebuilder, Stan. He was "starting a new world," he said, and we were "candidates" for it.

"Where are you building this new world?" Ralf asked.

David took a swig of wine and said, "Mystery."

"How do I know if I want to go then?" said Ralf, who invariably acted just as audacious around David as at any other time.

"I'll let you know when the time's right," David responded, a gleam in his eye.

Ralf and I each ordered a beer, and David went on to mention that he'd been to Marbella (a ritzy costal town west of Malaga).

"I've been meeting some interesting people down there," he said. "I met a sixty year-old English guy who was in a mystical school once."

"Are you thinking of moving there?" Ralf asked.

"Maybe someday," David said, finishing his wine and gesturing to the bartender for another.

"And we're invited?" Ralf asked hopefully.

"I said you were 'candidates.'"

"What means 'candidate?'" Ralf, whose English was more than passible but strangely 'off' or 'on,' inquired.

David turned to me. "Can you explain it to him professor?"

"It means we're being considered," I said.

BOOK II
BOULDER TO THE
BERKSHIRES AND BACK

CHAPTER 1

It was the summer of 1996. Over two years had passed since my return from Spain.

After considering my options, I had eventually gravitated back to Boulder and Colorado University, where I'd been studying before going to Spain. I was taking creative writing classes and working as a waiter at an inn. It seemed my life was returning to its old form.

From time to time, I had wondered if I would ever return to Spain. I assumed everyone there had forgotten about me, but then one day, out of the blue, Jane called.

Over the phone, her voice sounded much higher than I remembered it. There was a sweetness to it, and she didn't sound far away at all. To my surprise, I felt relaxed.

She asked what I was doing and I hesitantly told her I was back at CU.

"Do you have a girlfriend?" she asked.

"No," I said slowly.

"But you did, right?"

"Yeah, how did you know?"

"Kindler and I ran into your friend Dan—he's in Berlin now—and he told us you'd written."

I suspected Jane's call had been prompted by David and whatever he was doing at the moment. She acted nonchalant, but I knew she was feeling me out.

Eventually, she asked if I was still recapitulating. I said, "No."

"Are you still interested in it?"

"I guess so. I haven't felt it was something I could do on my own," I said.

"You're not alone. David says it doesn't matter if you're in America."

She talked about how it was Spring—time for a new beginning. "We're all here at the beach: David, me, Kindler, Paroana—You remember Paroana—and Liza. David's got a house. It's really paradise."

"Sounds great," I said.

She must have known my thoughts because she said, "Don't worry about the past. It's not important. David really likes you. He talks about you a lot."

Suddenly, I felt free for the first time in two years. I'd felt guilty about leaving Spain, and was sure I was somehow 'bad' in David's eyes.

"David says that if we both recapitulate every day, we'll have a real connection. He also said it will help the world."

"Wow," I said.

"Yeah."

I felt I could talk to Jane all day. "I feel like you're right here in my room," I said.

She laughed. "Yeah, me too."

Neither of us wanted to say goodbye. I said, "See you later, bye," about five times before finally hanging up the phone.

A few days later, she called again to see how my recapitulation was going. I told her it was okay, but that I wasn't sure if I was doing it right.

"It seems like the most important thing is the intent," I said. "I feel different afterwards, more centered, but I'm not having any grand revelations."

"Have you figured anything out?" she asked.

"I don't know. I've been working on envy. I've found that if I see my envy, it turns into hope."

"What was the envy and the hope?"

"It had to do with Kindler mostly," I said. "I was envious of his guitar-playing, but when I recapitulated it, I realized he taught me a lot."

"That's good. I've been working on Kindler too."

"What have you been working on?"

"Everything. How we wound up together. Lots of stuff."

She paused and I waited to see what she would say next.

"It's hard…" she said. "Some days I almost can't do it. Liza's been helping me a little."

"How is Liza?" I asked.

"She's doing really well. She reminds me a lot of Deliana. She's more like my older sister though."

"Really?"

"Yeah, it was a little strange at first seeing them together. I'm used to it now. Liza's more like my older sister though."

Having made a connection to Jane and Spain, my life took on new meaning again. I felt I had something, that I belonged somewhere. I didn't have many friends in Boulder. I wasn't even very close with my roomates, but that didn't matter to me now. I began to notice that my attitude, the feeling of having something, made me more attractive to people. Most importantly, I didn't feel like a sinner anymore.

CHAPTER 2

"David won't talk to me anymore. He told me to call you and ask you what to do."

"About what?" I asked.

"He said I can't make it without you. When Kindler and I found out we couldn't be together anymore, he said, 'It doesn't matter, you don't need a man right now.' Now he says I can't make it without a man and that you and I are twin souls. So what should I do? Should I come to Boulder or what?"

I was in shock, but I was also pleased that Jane needed me.

"Would you want to come here?" I said.

Jane laughed. "I don't know."

"We'll figure out something," I said.

Jane had been in Spain for six years and I could tell that part of her wanted a break. I also knew that, even with David's blessing, the idea of coming back to America scared her. The two of us had really met and gotten to know each other in Spain. Even after just a few months there, we'd begun to associate our lives in America with different selves.

I had come to see our meeting one another as an event that had required special circumstances and possibly, as David might have said, the help of higher beings. In short, it had taken a 'third point' to bring us together, and the third point was Spain and David.

I wondered whether it would be possible for us to live according to our essences if we were both in America. It seemed like a situation that somehow just wasn't meant be be.

CHAPTER 3

The next time she called, she told me she had exciting news. David had decided we should meet in New York and go to *The Berkshires* together. His long-time friend, Phil, lived in New York and had agreed to let Jane and me stay with him and his family for awhile.

David had once lived in the Berkshires and worked in a recording studio there, that was the connection. For Jane and me, it would be a new place, with fresh possibilites. On the east coast, we would be that much closer to Spain, and we would have a connection to David, through Phil.

When I told my friend John I was driving to New York to meet Jane, he said, "I'm envious; it sounds so romantic." I quit my job at the inn, packed my car, and drove across the country in two days, sleeping at rest areas along the way for a few hours at a time.

When I told Jane, who was already at Phil's house, that I was two hours from the city, she said, "Wow, you got here fast." As I drove over The George Washington bridge, I couldn't believe that just two days before, I'd been waiting tables in Boulder. That life seemed so far away now. I marveled at how little it meant to me and how willing I'd been to give it up so easily.

CHAPTER 4

Jane was in the shower when I arrived at Phil's. Phil gave me a beer and told me to make myself at home. We sat for awhile with neither of us saying much. I wondered how he perceived all of this. What had David told him, and where did he fit in this story?

I knew that David never arranged anything without giving everyone a part. I suspected that he had certain hopes concerning Phil, but I wasn't sure what they were. Phil himself seemed a little uncertain as to what his role was.

Jane finally appeared. She looked like an elf—smaller and more delicate than I remembered her. The first thing she said to me was, "Wow, you're so big!"

I had indeed gained a few pounds since the last time we'd seen each other, but I certainly was not even close to what could be called fat. She was obviously disappointed with something in me, however, and this took away some of the excitement from our highly anticipated reunion.

To break the ice, we went to a nearby bar for drinks. Jane was obviously experiencing culture shock. "Seinfeld," one of my favorite shows, was on the T.V. She of course had never heard of the show.

"So, how've you been?" I said

"I'm in shock," she confirmed. "I'm glad I'm here though. I'm sorry; it's just going to take a little while to get to know each other again."

I was disappointed that Jane hadn't been immediately attracted to me, but I told myself we'd eventually fall in love again.

CHAPTER 5

I had had only seventy-five dollars in my bank account in Boulder, and Jane of course had no money, so we decided to go to *The Berkshires* and look for work.

We pulled into Stockbridge in pouring rain with me singing the line from James Taylor's "Sweet Baby James": *So was the turnpike from Stockbridge to Boston...* Jane and I were finally starting to feel comfortable together. But our good mood slowly vanished when we couldn't find the campsite shown on the map and finally had to sleep in the car. I tried to joke about it, but Jane was clearly annoyed.

In the morning, we drove back into town and stopped for coffee at the first place on the main street, "The Red Lion Inn." As we sat on the porch, we felt out of place, like a couple of hippies surrounded by rich tourists. Jane began to complain about how we couldn't afford the two-dollar coffees. She asked how much money I had and when I told her, she said, "What are we going to do?"

"How hard can it be to find a job?" I said. "We've got to have faith we're in the right place."

"You're right," she said.

After finding nothing in the want ads, Jane said, "Why don't we ask here?"

The inn wasn't hiring we were told.

"Do you know of any place that might be?" I asked the clerk.

"No, sorry. This is a tourist town and most of the summer jobs are filled in March or even earlier," he said.

Feeling dejected, we sat down on one of the couches in the lobby.

"I don't believe that guy," Jane said. "You're too receptive."

"How am I too receptive?" I said defensively.

"It's just the way you are."

I felt she was comparing me to Kindler, who always had a way with people. I was angry, but I knew she was right. My body language, everything about me, said "Schmuck."

I knew what my problem was. I was afraid of rejection. I acted nice so that people would act nice to me. What I needed was to be *ruthless*.

Ruthlessness with myself meant not caring what anyone thought of me.

I walked up to the clerk at the front desk and said, "Hi, it's me again. Listen, is there another manager I can talk to about a position here in the hotel?"

"You're welcome to fill out an application if you like, but as I already told you, there are no positions available right now."

Just then, a tall, well-dressed woman happened to walk by and overhear what the clerk had said. "What kind of position are you looking for?" she said.

"Anything. My girlfriend and I…"

"There's two of you?" she said. Looking over at Jane, she asked, "What are you doing here in Stockbridge?"

I said something about reconnecting and making a fresh start.

"Hmm, rekindling an old relationship?" she said skeptically.

Realizing I'd already given away too much information, I tried to recover by saying, "We just like it here, and we want to live here for the summer."

"Why here?" she said.

Not wanting to make the same mistake again, I said, "We just heard it was nice here, so we came, and…"

"You decided to stay."

"Yeah."

"Well, I need some help downstairs in "The Lion's Den." I might be able to hire you both. Do you have any experience?"

I told the woman, who's name was Elena, that I'd been working at an inn in Boulder, and that I'd worked in restaurants before.

"Why don't you both come at 4:00 tomorrow. You can start tomorrow night."

I told Jane that meeting Elena was a sign we were in the right place.

That afternoon, we went swimming at *Stockbridge Bowl* and looked for David's old recording studio. We didn't find the studio, but we did find a nice campsite in Lee, the next town over.

The next morning, we went to a cafe the campsite manager had recommended. To our surprise, Elena was there with her daughter.

"What a coincidence," I said.

"Stockbridge is a small town," Elena said.

I didn't say anything, but I knew Jane was thinking the same thing I was: It was another sign.

Jane and Elena hadn't officially met yet, so I introduced them.

"What a cute couple you guys are!"

Elena told us she'd lived in Stockbridge most of her life and I could see that Jane was tempted, as I was, to ask her if she'd known David.

Instead, we asked if she knew the recording studio. We said we'd heard about it from our friend Phil in New York.

"Yeah, I know it. It's actually in West Stockbridge. *The Shaggy Dog*, right? I don't think it's a recording studio anymore."

Along with San Francisco, Stockbridge was the place David referred to most when talking about his past. He would want to know what had happened to the studio and we felt it was our duty to find out all we could.

"Why are you so interested in that place?" Elena asked.

Jane, not able to hold back anymore, said, "We know someone who used to work there. He's about your age."

Hearing the name, Elena said, "I think I know him." But her inability to recall anything specific about David made me wonder if she was being truthful. I could tell Jane was a little disappointed.

Elena had paid for her breakfast. "I'm on my way to work now. I have to take care of some things, but I'll see you at 4:00, right?"

"Right, see you then," I said.

CHAPTER 6

On our way back to the campsight, Jane said, "So what do you think of Elena?"

"I don't know, she's okay. Why?"

"The way she was looking at you. Didn't you notice?"

This was typical of Jane. After an encounter in which she'd been uncomfortable, she often resorted to blame. I'd gotten to understand this about her and now, instead of telling her she was being unreasonable, I took her behavior as a wake-up signal, a sign something wasn't 'kosher.'

David had often said that Jane, as an Aries, couldn't keep her mouth shut. She had to talk. I, on the other hand, almost never spoke up when things seemed off.

Instead of arguing with Jane, I let her vent.

Finally, she began she calm down. "Aren't you going to say anything?" she said.

"We can't change her," I began, "unless we change something in ourselves first. David said if you can control yourself, you can control others."

"But I don't feel like there's anything wrong with us," she said.

"We must have something in us that's like her," I said, "otherwise there would be no need to blame."

"You're right!" Jane said. It seemed she'd had a revelation.

I continued, "You see something in her you don't like; you know you have it in you too somewhere, and you start to pick it apart, pick her apart, and externalize whatever that thing is. That's what blame is. Even if you're right, you end up losing energy. There's a better way to be."

"What's that?"

I felt a lightbulb come on in my head. "Forgive her."

Jane started to cry. I told her it was okay; she'd helped me see something I'd never understood before.

"What's that?" she asked.

"I understand recaptulation a little better."

Putting my arm around her, I said, "You make it practical because you're such a blame-machine." This made her laugh.

"I am not."

"Okay, you're a barometer."

"What's that?"

.

CHAPTER 7

While we waited for 4:00 to roll around, we went to what we now referred to as the swimming hole.

We found a secluded area and decided to skinny-dip. I flattered Jane by calling her a water nymph and as we splashed in the water, we both felt like kids.

As we lay on the sun-drenched rocks, I tried to 'steal kisses' from her. Although she wasn't completely receptive to my attempts, neither did she seem offended in any way. This inter-play seemed so natural that I wondered why I'd never experienced it before. I'd always had trouble approaching girls because of my fear of rejection. Now, finding myself in an inno-cent, or essential, state, I realized that I didn't have that fear.

David had once said that the act of making love starts with instinct. He had also told me when we met, and I found this to be true, that my instinct was messed up. It seemed to me that a healthy instinct was connected to essentialness. Kids, before they hit puberty and begin to accrue all kinds of sexual imprints, are innocent. Another thing that is true about kids is that they always know what they want. I understood this to be a function of instinct.

It occurred to me that what I was experiencing now was 'foreplay.' I'd never thought of foreplay as being necessary to the process of making love. I was a late bloomer and by the time I hit puberty, I had been conditioned to think only about the end result, getting laid.

I could see how, as a teenager, peer pressure, and fear of not 'measuring up' had destroyed my instinct. For instance, I had often pursued girls that were not my type. Even in college, I had dated girls that I wasn't really attracted to. I was with them because I was trying to impress my friends, or because my ego said I needed a girlfriend.

I recalled how, in discussing *octaves*, one of the things David had talked about was the importance of making a right beginning. It seemed to me that in making love, the right beginning was: What happens when one finds oneself sitting next to a pretty girl on a rock by a lake, not: The immediate fixation on a hoped-for conclusion upon spotting a pretty girl across a smoke-filled bar (not that I have anything against bars).

Just as 'the octave of making love' doesn't start with the act of intercourse, it doesn't end with 'climax.' Rather, at that point, a new octave begins. How the new octave proceeds depends upon the 'level of vibration' reached in the previous octave.

CHAPTER 8

The topic of conversation on the way to our 4:00 p.m. meeting with Elena was money.

"We're down to our last thirty-five dollars," I said.

"Do you think we can ask Elena for an advance?" Jane asked.

"Let's wait and see," I said. She hasn't even officially hired us yet."

As soon as we walked into Elena's office, I could tell something was wrong. Elena looked serious for the first time since we'd met.

"I've decided I'm not going to hire you both," she said. "I just don't think it'll work, having a couple work together."

She gave us a moment to let the 'news' sink in, then asked me, "Do you still want the job?"

I didn't tell her we were almost out of money and had no choice.

"Yeah—I mean yes," I said.

I filled out the W4 paperwork while Jane waited in the lobby.

"Do you know how to carry a tray?" Elena asked.

"Yeah, I've done it before," I said. This was partially true. In the job I'd held for two weeks in Boulder, we'd practiced carrying trays with plates on them, no food. In the little experience I'd had serving customers, I hadn't had to carry heavy trays; we had usually brought the food out one or two plates at a time.

I would need black pants and black shoes Elena told me. "The Lion's Den" would provide a polo shirt.

"Can you be here a six tomorrow morning?"

"Sure," I said.

"Okay, see you then."

"Did you ask her about the advance?" Jane asked.

"Not yet," I said.

"Why not?"

I said it hadn't been the right time to ask; I hadn't wanted to risk not getting the job. "She already changed her mind about hiring us both," I added.

CHAPTER 9

The $9.50 I spent at a thrift store on pants and shoes left us with just enough money to pay our camping fees and to order two specials at "Joe's Diner," a mom and pop restaurant we'd discovered in Lee.

We both agreed that the food at Joe's was made with love and felt lucky to have found the place, but we were getting tired of eating at restaurants all the time. Jane was longing to cook a real meal.

"We need an apartment," she said.

"I agree, but right now, we need to think about how we're going to eat tomorrow."

I'd been in this situation before, many times in fact; while living in Spain. I'd learned how to ask for credit at the bars and restaurants that knew me. One or two liked me well enough to let me run a tab for days or even weeks at a time. I'd handled the humiliation of being reduced to this condition by repeating to myself something I'd read in one of George Gurdjieff's books. "In the real world, everyone is a beggar," he'd said.

The most important lesson I learned through my experiences with borrowing had to do with trust. When someone gave me credit, they were investing their faith in me. Sometimes the bartender or restaurant owner would say "No" initially, but if I told him, "Te pago mannana, seguro," he would reluctantly agree. When I showed up the next day to pay my debt, I would invariably be greeted by someone who was pleasantly surprised and I would leave knowing the person had become more trusting because his faith had been rewarded.

But it was one thing to ask for credit for myself and quite another to ask for both Jane and me. I didn't know what to do. *There must be another way,* I thought as I finished my plate of spaghetti.

I thought of calling my parents to ask for money, but that too meant losing face. Besides, they'd already said "No" once.

I was thinking about going to work the next morning on an empty stomach when I suddenly remembered I still had a check coming to me from my job in Boulder. Maybe that money would tide us over until my first paycheck.

I arranged to have the check mailed to me, but it would take a few days.

In the meantime, we ate on credit, assuring the storekeepers and restaurant owners a check was on its way. We stayed away from the campground as much as possible so the manager wouldn't ask us to pay our daily fees.

I worked mornings and evenings at "The Lion's Den." I'd been given the job of runner, which meant picking up the food from the kitchen and bringing it downstairs to the back area of "The Den." We rarely got very busy and apart from almost dropping the heavy tray a couple times, things went fairly smooth.

CHAPTER 10

Each night at the campsite we built a fire.

After an hour or so, I would crawl into the tent Phil had loaned us; Jane usually followed within a few minutes. A couple times, lying there in the dark, I tried putting my arm around her. There was a palpable warmth between us, and I was merely acting on it, doing what came natural. But she continued to brush me off.

One night, I persisted more than usual and she got angry.

"Well, what's the matter?" I said. "I've been sleeping next to you every night for almost a week. When are you going to give it up?"

"I'm sorry," she said, her back turned to me. "I can't."

"Why not?"

"Because I'm still in love with Kindler."

"I think you just think you are," I said.

I hadn't anticipated our next problem.

I finally received the check, but there was no way to cash it as I didn't have a bank account. None of the stores would accept it.

I tried asking other customers at the bank to cash it for me…until the bank manager told me I would have to leave.

The only thing left to do was to ask Elena for help. We would have to wait another day though, as it was Saturday, her day off. I had the rest of the day off as well and having nothing else to do, we decided to do some exploring.

We'd passed the Kripalu Yoga Center several times on our way from Stockbridge to Lenox, a town just down the road. We decided to take a closer look.

Nothing much was going on when we got there; the place was empty.

We wandered around the building and the grounds, which sat atop a grassy hillside. There were pictures inside of people sitting on the grass meditating, big smiles on their faces. *The school of bliss*, I thought.

Apart from its pristine setting, I couldn't see or feel anything special about the place. *It's just another retreat for upper-class pseudo-spiritualites,* I thought.

We drove further down the road until we came to a kind of park. Off in the distance was some type of gray, stone structure. It drew my attention and I stopped the car and got out.

"Where are you going?" Jane asked.

"I'm going to take a look at this monument," I said. I had a sudden urge to run.

The dash across the grassy ravine, up the steep hillside, left me breathless. I stood panting, doubled over for a minute. Then I beheld the shrine. It was beautiful, the most stunning *Virgin Mary* I'd ever seen.

I'd never been particularly impressed by religious sculptures. In fact, I'd never seen one I would have called 'alive.' But this one was; I could even sense the presence of the sculptor somehow. I could tell the scupture had been created by a spiritual person who'd been in love at the time.

I told all of this to Jane when she finally reached the hilltop, but she didn't seem to be listening.

"What's wrong?" I said.

"I just feel like nothing is going right," she admitted. "I mean, we have no money, no plan. I have no job. I can't just depend on you to support us both."

I just looked at Jane. It made me sad that she only seemed to see the negative side of things. We'd had a lot of fun in the last week: Singing along with Bob Dylan and Bonnie Raitt while driving along the country roads from town to town; skinny-dipping in *The Bowl*; sitting in the glow of the campfire talking about the Grateful Dead; catching up with one another. It hurt me that none of this seemed to have meant anything to her. We'd only been together for a week and it already seemed like she was giving up. I knew it had been a shock for her just coming back to The States. *Maybe she is still in love with Kindler*, I thought. *Or maybe she just can't adjust to being here.*

The next morning, I discovered that my car was out of gas. It wouldn't even start. Without waking Jane, I walked into town. I explained my situation to the gas-station attendant, who finally agreed to 'loan' me a couple gallons of gas to get to work in Stockbridge.

When I showed up at "The Red Lion," I was two hours late. I had no choice but to try and explain things to Elena.

"So you guys are broke?" she said.

"Unless you could maybe give me an advance…?" I said.

"I'm sorry. I already gave you a job. I can't be loaning money to employees. What about your friend Phil?"

Phil was two hours away. Besides, he'd already put us up in his apartment and I hadn't wanted to trouble him anymore.

"Well, it's obvious that you guys have other things on your mind," Elena said. "I can't have people working for me if they can't even get here on time. I think you should go stay with your friend until you figure things out."

CHAPTER 11

I should have known right then that once we left *The Berkshires*, what little momentum we had would be lost.

We talked little on the way back to the city.

Phil cashed my check for me the night we got back and said we could continue to stay with him. It seemed possible to start over. We could think things out more carefully this time, and decide where to go next.

But Jane was brooding, practically ignoring me. I felt like a failure, even though I hadn't really done anything wrong. Or had I?

Phil asked Jane what was wrong and she announced that she wanted to be 'on her own' for awhile.

"What's awhile?" he asked.

"I don't know."

Phil, who was clearly enjoying the role of daddy that had suddenly been entrusted to him (after all, our fate had ended up in his hands), seemed to now be pondering the evidence before him, like the judge he must have always aspired to be (he was actually a lawyer). For a minute, he seemed torn, but then I felt my heart sink as I saw he was about to be taken in by the oldest trick in the book, "the damsel in distress."

"I'll support whatever you decide to do," he said. "Where do you want to go?"

"I'll stay at the youth hostel in the city," Jane said.

"What'll you do for money?"

"I can get my friend Sandra to send me some," she said.

I felt the last remnants of my manhood slip away. Phil had had the power to convince Jane to stick to the plan, which was for me and her to stay together. He had been given a job by David, but he'd chosen to 'follow' Jane; I was sure this was how David would have perceived the situation. I could see that Phil felt he was being nice and that he'd somehow convinced himself that was his job.

I'd had my chance though, and I'd somehow blown it. I hadn't said or done the right things at the right time; I hadn't trusted myself enough. I'd even allowed feelings of inadequacy and self-pity to get in the way of what Jane and I were doing together. Jane's not being in love with me hadn't bothered me that much until the last day or so, but now it seemed like the final straw. *There's no point in sticking around anymore*, I told myself. *It's over.*

I packed my car and prepared to leave, even though it was night-time and I had over 2000 miles to drive.

"Wait," Jane said. "Don't leave yet."

She got in the car with me and we sat in silence for a few minutes.

"I want to keep in touch with you. I feel bad that you came all this way and it didn't work out. I thought things would be different. I can't help that I'm still in love with Kindler."

"Are you really in love with him," I said, "or is it just more comfortable to be with him?"

"I'm really in love with him."

BOOK III
A CHOICE

CHAPTER 1

Three and a half years had passed since I'd last seen David. I continued to think of him a lot, and wondered what he was doing. In dreams, I saw him working on a guitar, writing, doing something with a house.

There were other people around, a new group. I couldn't make out all their faces. There was a girl in a Japanese kimono who vaguely resembled Jane. I saw Phil too, only he wasn't in Spain; he was floating over The Atlantic, as if part of him had remained in limbo all this time.

The three and a half years, outward changes notwithstanding, signified something else, at least according to David. It signified when we all took a 'crucial turn' in our evolutions; where we'd all decided to remain unconscious instead of waking up.

In my case, I was quite happy. I was working as a graphic artist now, having gone through a one-year training program. It had taken twenty-nine years, but I finally had a career. I had almost quit the program once, but I'd finally graduated and found the perfect job.

Looking back, I would wonder why I'd been so willing to 'pull up stakes' and leave the country again when David contacted me by email that early February.

One must understand that David represented perfection to me. I still had the words he'd said to me early on in our relationship, ten years before, when I'd been trying to decide whether to stay in Spain or not, ringing in my ears: "All you have to decide is whether you want to be a Superman or a normal schmuck."

It seemed to me, when David contacted me, that life was asking me, again: "*Superman or normal schmuck?*"

For years, I had wondered whether the 'old gang' would ever get together again. Just when I thought it would never be, I got the call. I should have known that our leader would be the one to initiate it.

I didn't say "Yes" at first. Although the majority of my correspondence with David, from the moment he 'found me,' had been positive, friendly even, I had complained from the get-go about "how things went down the last time I was there."

David's reply was: "It's no use blaming God." Rather than reacting defensively to this statement, I somehow 'took it'; I felt the truth in David's words and not only took back what I'd said, but even made some long promises about helping to 'make things right.'

I was told I could help make Nerja, David's town, paradise, raise the sail on the old trusty ship so to speak.

"The others will be back," David promised. "Maybe sooner than you think."

Despite my strong positive feeling about David, I went back and forth for a month on whether to go or not. I weighed the pros and cons daily. Ultimately, though, I realized that the decision wasn't, and couldn't be, a mental one.

One morning in early March, I woke up with the knowledge that I had passed the point of no return. I had made my choice. I was going.

CHAPTER 2

When I arrived at the door to David's shop, part of me wondered whether I was really there. Technically, David and I hadn't actually spoken in what seemed like forever, but the first thing out of his mouth, "Hey, email works!" confirmed what I was feeling, that we'd somehow been connected all this time.

David looked the same: same long, graying hair, same corduroy pants and flannel top, same stance, same gaze, same smile. I immediately noticed though—he looked *dusty*. His hair, even the shop had...the image that occurred to me was a sort of "out in the desert for forty years" feel. I couldn't help feeling a twinge of pity.

"Hey, where are you staying?" David asked me.

"Hostal Alhambra," I said.

"Beautiful. Let's get some coffee. There's a nice little plaza over there. I bet it's pretty cool seeing the ocean again, huh?"

"Yeah," I said.

David snatched his wallet and shoulder bag from the table by the door, performed his ritualistic 'pocket-check' ("Keys, cash— *'It's Euros now'*—cigarettes, silver dollar). "Okay, vamos. Hey, it's nice to see you," he added, closing the shop door.

The plaza was almost empty as we settled into our chairs. The waiter, who'd been standing in the doorway of the nearby cafe and who recognized David, came over.

"Buenas tardes! Que quereis tomar?"

David ordered a *"Cortado."*

"I switched about a year ago," he said. "More espresso, less milk."

As we waited for the drinks, David related to me how he and Deliana had stayed at "Hostal Alhambra" their first time in Nerja, fifteen years before.

We're off to a good start, I thought.

"What movie did they show on the plane? There's always a movie, right?" David asked me.

"Yeah, uhm, *Pay it Forward,*" I said with a chuckle.

"Any good?"

"Yeah, I mean…"

"Tell me."

"Well, this kid, Halley Joel Osmond," I began.

"Donnie Osmond's son?" David dead-panned.

"No. C'mon," I said. "No, it's about a kid who decides to change the world or something by doing good things for his mom, his teacher…he basically connects his mom and his teacher. He basically wants his teacher to be his dad," I finished.

"Sounds groovy," David said. "See, we're right back where we were the last time you were Eric."

David's words, as always, were encouraging, but a little biting. "That's okay," I told myself, David's David. Anyway, the important thing is, I'm here."

I rolled a Drum cigarette and thought to myself that the Costa del Sol air was so balmy and dewy-sweet, I almost didn't have to lick the paper. I chuckled at this "Seinfeld" riff, thought about sharing it with David, then, going back to the *Pay it Forward* conversation and my last association with it, said, "You know, my father passed away recently."

David's nonplussed reaction told me right away this wasn't new news to him. Nevertheless, he said gently, "How old *was* he?"

"He was almost sixty," I said holding back tears.

David did not confirm outright that he had known about my father's death, but I knew that he had, and I knew there was more to his knowing than he was likely to admit. In my relationship with David, there had been times when he'd denied, played down at least, his own 'omniscience.' I remembered him saying to me once, half-kidding, "I might know everything, but you still have to fill me in on the details!" I had to admit that I understood, even shared, David's sentiments in this regard. *Maybe too much information could be a drag*, I thought.

Pulling myself back into the moment and changing the subject, I asked David how *his* life was.

CHAPTER 3

David related the story of how he had called *Rolling Stone* with what he'd called "The Story of the Century" and been rudely hung up on. Apparently, his 'pitch' hadn't made it past the secretary. He'd written a story—it was the beginning of a book—about the experience and said he would show it to me; it was back at the shop.

The story, *E=mc^2, You Just Feel It,* was hilarious, sweet, and smart; I read it over and over as I lay in my bed at the hostal each night. I knew David was a writer, but this latest piece inspired me like no piece of writing I'd read, at least not since Castaneda, and truth be told, David's story really *was* 'gold.'

David shared with me many other stories—short stories—he'd written. One, "The Baron Von Barcelona" was particularly insightful and funny. The story was about him and Liza, and Liza's family and how they perceived Liza's being with David. At one point, David had found—in a dumpster near his shop—some old stocks from a defunct transportation company in Barcelona. He had then tried—or pretended to try—to sell the 'phony' stocks to Liza's dad. A big part of the story, I thought, had to do with arrogance, or self-importance.

I particularly liked the story's 'turn,' where the uptight "Swiss Minister," as David calls him, discovers that "The crazy American," far from being some sort of inept thief, is really just playing him, repaying him his snobbish attitude of: "Who do you think you are to date my daughter?" He—the American—doesn't *have* to do what he does; as another David piece says, "(It's) not necessary; it's free." But the stocks do *represent* something, and by the end of the story, the Swiss family is half-convinced they're real!

I rolled with laughter the first half-dozen times I read "The Baron Von Barcelona." Finally, I asked David if he still had the stocks; sure enough, he did. They were perfectly official-looking and for a cool one hundred Euros I acquired a very stylish piece of memorabilia for my wall! I also felt rewarded for 'supporting the arts' as David called it.

CHAPTER 4

I found a one-bedroom apartment on *Calle Cristo*, on the other side of town from David's shop. There was a horrible stench; I seriously wondered if someone had died there. I burned incense constantly and finally the smell faded somewhat. As I got used to the apartment, the neighborhood, and to the feeling of being in Spain again, I began to feel like I almost belonged here.

Once again, I was a little surprised at my willingness to leave my old life (job, family, routines, surroundings). On the other hand though, it was exhilarating to be in what felt like a new place (I'd never really lived at the beach before). I'd come with one large backpack. It—the backpack—made me think of a dream I'd once had where someone had told me, "Pack your life up—you've got five minutes."

"C'mon, it's time," the voice had then said. Of course, I hadn't even known how to begin.

As I look back on my arrival—alone—in Nerja, where I'd had only a vague idea of what to expect, then finding the apartment and making peace with my decision to come, I still recall how one minute I'd been terrified, overwhelmed by the unknown, then, seemingly just a minute later, my body and mind had somehow accepted everything and a warm feeling of security had come over me. I'd experienced this transistion before, but it had never seemed so swift, like moving a set of suitcases from one side of the room to another.

I went to a nearby electronics store and bought a portable CD player. I met a couple of my neighbors. Every morning, David and

I had rolls and coffee at "The German Bakery," a little breakfast place around the corner from his shop which stayed open until 3:00 or 4:00 in the afternoon.

David called his writing operation—his stories, his book, and the emails he sent out from the *Med Web Internet Cafe*—"The Axarquian Sun." He joked that he felt like Clark Kent, as he toiled anonymously at 2:00 or 3:00 in the morning at the cafe, which was open all night.

The story of how David had discovered the internet was even more knee-slapping. He'd been standing in the middle of the street—right outside the *Med Web* as luck would have it— complaining aloud, or to the person he was with, that a certain important letter he was awaiting still hadn't arrived.

"The mail in Spain is so f————— slow! What'da they use? Burros?" he'd screamed.

A man standing nearby, overhearing, and perhaps laughing to himself, said, "Hey, buddy, you know they've got this thing called The Internet now. You can send mail just about anywhere and it gets there right away."

The rest was history. David became, by his own admission, "a computer nerd," almost overnight it seemed. By the time I arrived, David was showing *me*, me who had just spent two and a half years studying graphic design, computer tricks and shortcuts.

"Want to burn a CD? Here, check out the video on this website!"

Of course, I had a few tricks up my sleeve too, and so we traded knowledge, sent out David's story as he added more chapters to it, and experimented with internet people-search techniques we hadn't yet tried.

CHAPTER 5

It was around the time when our people-search petered out (I had made contact with Jane, but she had emphatically declined my offer to "Come on over, get a tan, have a milk-shake"), that my routine began to change. Instead of meeting David faithfully at "The German Bakery" each morning, I started making frequent treks into the countryside, or to Maro, a village up the road. Something—my own thoughts?—was drawing me there.

I had a history of bipolar illness, and had experienced several 'manic flights' before. It didn't take much, I had learned, to kick off one of these supernormal 'adventures' (David's term). A switch went on, I began seeing things, hearing things, and finally, entering into altered states of consciousness which could last days, weeks, even months.

Some of my doings during this time included accosting a group of German tourists (I yelled at one man, "Hey, Einstein," and accused him of inventing the atomic bomb), confronting the Swedish owners of the *Med Web Cafe* with the message that I was the antichrist, and losing my passport, wallet, notebooks, and apartment keys somewhere along the country road between Nerja and Maro.

All of these activities, though far from harmless, were, until now, more or less 'par for the course.' I had never been around David during these times; I was off in Madrid the first time, where

I'd managed to steal a taxi, get thrown in jail, hitch-hike halfway back to Granada with a black eye and, of course, no money...the stories were horrific all.

Due to my manic state, or, more likely, due to the combination of *my* heightened awareness and David's reaction to it as a higher being himself, our breakfast on the morning of my third—or was it my fourth? —return from Maro was strained, apocyliptic even.

David made me give him my credit card, upon which we went to the ATM nearby; I had to show David how to use it (he'd never used plastic before in his life). After handing over two hundred fifty Euros for the 'trouble' I'd put him through (David called it balancing the budget), we tried to get into my apartment, which was, of course, locked.

The entire morning, the urgency, intensity, and fear I was experiencing (all hallmarks of a severe manic episode) steadily increased. At a certain point, I felt that David's intensity, far from distilling my own symtoms, was exacerbating them. On the way back from my apartment, I was convinced that something awful was imminent. I saw repeated images of David ripping my arm off; I heard voices saying I needed to kill someone; I felt I was practically exploding from the inside.

We finally ended up in the middle of Plaza Isabel, the geographic center of town. As we stood there, the panic that had been mounting within me suddenly crescendoed into an overwhelming pressure of death. I looked out across town, at the long series of streets leading to the carretera, and heard myself say, "No, way too far." I grabbed David by the collar in a desperate 'fight response'; David simply turned my arm and put me to the ground, holding me there for a few seconds, then letting me go.

No sooner had I regained my feet, I began racing towards the wall of the beachside walkway, some 100 meters away. I hopped over the six-foot wall in one motion, bounded down to the beach, stripped down, as I ran, to my underwear, and, placing my watch, shoes, and hat on the nearest rock I could find, hit the surf, swimming vigorously into the sea as voices, images of whales, and a monumental life-or-death surge of energy propelled me.

Those who have never felt unbearable pressure of death do not, *cannot* in my opinion, even begin to understand what drives a human being to suicide. No one—again, in *my* opinion—*wants* to die.

This was not a suicide attempt. Beyond the 'choice' of returning to Spain (to be a 'Superman' — okay, an admittedly lofty aim), I had no control whatsoever over what happened that fateful morn.

CHAPTER 6

The world (my doctors, the lawyer who sent me to the state hospital, my own family even) would scoff at my 'delusion' that I could survive by projecting my consciousness—not astral-projecting, as that requires *AIR*—into the body of a whale.

That didn't happen, but I did survive. The coast-guard, I found out some time later, had fished me out of the sea. I woke up in a Malaga hospital, i.v.s and tubes attached here and there, a good half-dozen or so quarts of sea-water in my stomach that I had to throw up, and a team of nurses who seemed curiously unsurprised at my revival.

I spent nine tortuous days at a psychiatric facility, where patients were indiscriminately given morning and evening doses of liquid haldol (same dose for everyone). Torturous because the dose, the drug, the way it was given, was wrong. I did the 'haldol shuffle' and foamed at the mouth the entire day, each day (when I wasn't entirely catatonic—again, from the drug). I was able to rise above the hell I was in, if only for minutes at a time, thanks to a spunky fellow patient, Belen, who engaged me in conversation and even some horseplay (we sparred with one another on the grassy court-yard outside).

Finally, my mom and brother showed up one morning. Even in my half-catatonia, I could see the worry on their faces as they approached me (I happened to be sitting in the same grassy area of the courtyard, with Belen).

My brother would later confess that, in the first few moments he'd witnessed me, *Brain damage!* had crossed his mind. His and my mother's worry continued until I began showing signs of my self later that evening, at the hotel they had booked for the night.

I made it through the long flight back from Madrid to Denver the next day.

I made it through the eight weeks—three of them spent entirely indoors—of hospitalization I underwent upon return. And I made it through the months of almost constant anxiety following my apparent near-drowning and the ensuing trama of the state hospital (unsympathetic, unbelieving, even callous, hospital staff, psychotic, occasionally violent fellow patients, and the general anxiety of being locked up).

Some weeks later, sitting in my brother Jon's livingroom, Jon would say to me, "You're the strongest person I know."

BOOK IV
RECOVERY

CHAPTER 1

My decision to participate in *Windhorse Community Services*, a wellness program for people with mental illness, was initially nothing more than a way of avoiding yet another state hospital commitment.

It was May, 2003 and I was back in Boulder again. I chose Windhorse in part because of Boulder. Having spent a good part of the last six years in the Rocky Mountain region, I felt it really was home. I'd felt very connected to Boulder even during my three-year stint in Spain.

My Windhorse 'team,' which consisted of a psychiatrist, therapist, several 'basic attendees,' (a program concept), and even a 'med team' (a group of mostly female staff who monitored my nightly med-taking) were graduates, or at least affiliates all, of Naropa University (a Buddhist school dating back to the early seventies).

From the beginning of my affiliation with *Windhorse*, I envisioned our partnership—probably due to the continuing influence of my Spain school—as more of a, yes, 'school,' than a recovery program. I, of course, was the teacher; my so-called 'providers,' students. Whether this vision had any basis in reality would depend, I suppose, on one's viewpoint.

By my second month with *Windhorse*, I had basically gotten to know each of the six men and women I worked with, seven including my therapist, eight including my doctor. The majority of the 'shifts' (another program concept) were spent taking photographs together, hitting the links (I helped shape several of my shift-partners' golf swings), strolling down Pearl Street, visiting cafes. The format of my *Windhorse* interactions was so loose (indeed, *Windhorse* themselves had designed it that way) that it would have been almost impossible to say, at least in an overall sense, who was learning from whom.

"We all learn from each other. Life is learning." Right, sure.

CHAPTER 2

By summer, the fact that I was paying *Windhorse* "beaucoup bucks," basically because of a verbal contract with the director made back in April when I'd been desperate to escape hospitalization and agreed to "stick with *Windhorse* for at least six months," wouldn't have bothered me so much, had the team leader and director not resisted so strongly when I decided to move on, quit the program.

"Why quit?" they said.

Why indeed? The people themselves were awesome; in another world, they would certainly have been friends. In the mental health world, however, there are certain hard and fast rules about 'getting too close.' It's a shame in one way....

On a purely practical level, I had been trying to get back to work—unsuccessfully, as my resume was full of holes and didn't scream, "Look at me!" My *Windhorse* team, well-intentioned though they were, were unfortunately not very helpful to this process. That was "Why."

Finally, though, while sitting on my front porch one late-June morn, Marta, perhaps without even knowing it, 'struck gold.'

"Have you heard of Chinook?" Marta said.

"Nun-uh," I grumbled.

"Well, a couple people I've worked with go there," she said. "They help people with jobs sometimes."

"Yeah?" I perked up.

"Yeah. The jobs aren't very specialized, but…"

"Jobs?" I said, "as in…like…those things where you get *paid* to do things, maybe even meet people too?" I half-kidded.

"Yeah," Marta said.

"Well, lead the way then!"

The next day, Marta drove me to *Chinook Clubhouse*. We toured the facility, and…

EPILOGUE

"So…*Chinook Clubhouse* is a social and vocational rehabilitation program for adults with mental illness," the director, Allan Guitar, explained. "I started this clubhouse in 1991 after attending a week-long Clubhouse conference in Massachusettes."

Thus began the second—if not the first—most significant episode of my life.

In my first two years at *Chinook*, I attended two major conferences myself, spent a year as the editor of the house newsletter, worked as an intern at "The Daily Camera," Boulder's main newspaper, stocked shelves at the CU library, participated in approximately two dozen public service presentations on mental illness and the Clubhouse Program,* served on Chinook's Advisory Board, and collaborated with the Colorado Clubhouse Association, a network of five Clubhouses in Colorado which promotes the Clubhouse mission and organizes local conferences and public relations events.

Most importantly though, I made tons of friends, perhaps even gave hope to a few fellow Clubhouse 'colleagues,' staff, and 'young minds' who attended the various presentations.

Hey, it beats school.

*To learn about "The Clubhouse Movement," go to your nearest internet cafe (unless you have a home computer) and visit ww.iccd.org" and/or "chinookclubhouse.org."